New Famous Phrases strikes with precision and purpose, bringing an ancient power to modern language. It feels as though Daniel Hinds has uncovered a hidden word-hoard, and with every line, the poems cut through to the truth. Reinventing the line-initial capitalization, these poems reshape tradition with controlled force. Every w[...] [...]
a lasting mark on the mind of
— Professor David Morley

CW01499643

In *New Famous Phrases*, Dar[...] [...]
the word-hoard. Classic the[...] [...]:
Apollo becomes the god of moonboots and red[...] a
mischievous magpie. Come and revel in the rites of spring, voyage with a young mariner, and enjoy innovative review-responses to contemporary voices. *New Famous Phrases* brims with freshness and virtuosity.
— Dr Yvonne Reddick

Erudite, witty, visionary and humorous, this is a collection of unexpected swerves in dialogue with the 'submerged voices' of poetry's bloodline. Blending song and story, this collection brings us inventive prose poem book reviews alongside insightful lyrics and fresh takes on mythology. Partly a testament to the artform itself, *New Famous Phrases* demonstrates a unique flair for sound and language. Hinds' ability to turn a phrase transforms perspective.
— Dr John Challis

New Famous Phrases is a sophisticated debut collection of poems that quirkily blend lyricism with a dialogic approach. These intense and dense poems, layered like geological memories and mindscapes, are inhabited by a multitude of conjured ghosts (from Dante and Shelley to W.S. Graham), inviting a conversation with the dead.
— Dr Ágnes Lehóczky

NEW FAMOUS PHRASES

Daniel Hinds is a poet from Newcastle. He is a BBC New Creative, Ilkley Literature Festival New Northern Poet, and New Writing North North East Poet. He won the Poetry Society's Timothy Corsellis Young Critics Prize. His poetry was commended in the National Centre for Writing's UEA New Forms Award, and has been broadcast on BBC platforms, performed at the Cockpit Theatre, and published in magazines, anthologies, and newspapers, including *The London Magazine, The New European, Wild Court, Southword,* and *Poetry Salzburg Review.*

ISBN: 978-1-916938-83-0

Cover designed by Aaron Kent

Edited and Typeset by Aaron Kent

Broken Sleep Books Ltd
PO BOX 102
Llandysul
SA44 9BG

Contents

THE PACT OF WATER   9

NINE SPILT YOLKS   10

JULEBUKKING   15

CRYPTID (THE MYSTERY OF WATER)   16

ODE TO A MAGPIE / ONE FOR SORROW   18

THE CRYING OF THE GULLS   19

EARTH GIANT   20

DEAR SYDNEY GRAHAM   22

I HAUNT YOU BACK   25

THE TRAIN GOES BACKWARDS   26

THE FIFTH SEASON   27

THE RITE OF WINTER   28

THE SIREN STAR   30

ODE TO APOLLO 11   32

KEEPING WATCH   34

THE CORONA PRINCE   36

THE EXPECTED OCCUPANT   39

SUNDOG HOWL   42

PHILIP PULLMAN'S GRADUATION   44

MAGPIE'S BIRDBATH   47

WINTER   48

THE GOBLIN   49

THE LESSER GOD PAN   50

EPIMETHEUS ON HIS CRAG   51

A PROSE POEM BOOK REVIEW   52

LADY OF THE ROCK   56

TWICE THE MAN   58

DEATH BY EARTH   61

STEPS TO ENGRAVEN THE EARTH   62

THE MAGI'S CAMEL   64

THE SEA CHAIN   66

SIREN'S THROAT   67

A GUIDE TO THE STONES   69

ANEIRIN   70

THE FOOTMAN.   72

PROSE / POEM   76

A BANQUET FOR PENELOPE   77

LIONESS AND PORTCULLIS   84

THE FIRST MAN   87

THE LAST ANIMAL   89

THE GREY RHINO   91

UNTITLED, THE FOURTH MONSTER   93

ENGLISH SOCIOPATH, OR, THE INSIDES OF A CUFFLINK BOX [...]   98

ACEDIA   102

THE YOUNG MARINER   104

THE DREAM OF METHUSELAH   106

SCRAPS TO DAUB A SIREN'S LIPS   108

ACKNOWLEDGEMENTS   111

New Famous Phrases

Daniel Hinds

Broken Sleep Books

THE PACT OF WATER

A bargain was struck
Like the wet smiting of a storm upon a shore.

They signed in a squirt of squid ink spray.
Our pen tip crossed the white threshold.

We looked up to them, those gods in cockle
And sea bone suits, shining upon the crest
Of a tsunami wave of Atlantean awe.

We hockled our liquid libation in their drink
And the slick grease of our phlegm spread.

Put your ear to a stone shell or a seal's black flank,
Hear the submerged voices raised in the world's blood.

Now we look down in meropian blindness,
Discern no cities capped beneath blue braes.

We let the water fall through our hands.
It leaves a tentacle pucker mark.

NINE SPILT YOLKS

From the speckled hen nine eggs I stole
— Dora Sigerson Shorter, *The Fairy Changeling*

I

Something I'll never know
Was stolen right out from under my tongue.

And in its place I unfurled
A soggy paper fairy child.

Some scrap of fallen faerie wisdom
That babbles like a baby, pretending to be a man,
Or a brook, pretending to be a steaming pot
Growing hot upon the hearth.

II

Paper child,

Your infant call keeps me awake all night.
I swaddle you in white robes, share in the second sight
Of your apposition eyes. Sometimes, I ignore your bawling,
Roll over, rest, and regret the blank page come morning,

When I can no longer see by day's decaying light
Whatever strange and sickle shape you held.

Other times, the gift is just a goblin
Gobbledegook trick. You laugh and leave me
A hex: untranslatable fayerye talk
Hoaxed on browning leaves,

Curling, like a monument to burnt parchment.

III

Sometimes, I scrub the muck off of you
And you disintegrate
In the bathtub

As if I'd boiled you with the eggshells.

When the dirty tub water transforms into a Naiad's laughter,
It's easy to throw the baby out with the bathwater.

IV

You're lucky you weren't born in a grimmer wooded age,
When witches and woodcutters wandered
The swallowed, beaten, breadcrumb path;
When some rustic rhymer would have gathered
Logs, and courage, and poverty's hungry unnamed
Necessity – and thrown you into the flames.

Now, more likely,
A wastepaper basket –
Squash you up squirming
And still shrill jabbering
With my other aborted litter.

Next day, lift you out,
Uncrease your little wrinkled body,
Hold you up to my loving breast

And interrogating eyes.

V

Infant migrant of Tuatha Dé Danann,
The girlish boyish wailing go-between,
The child of two worlds.

VI

Sum of all my days, I waste before
Your unending appetite for my life,
My thoughts, my loves, my dreams.

Sometimes I wear the seams inside
Out so you can't get to me
With your suckling screams.

Your pudgy pixie hands have an iron grip,
But I know you fear the cut of iron scissors

And judicious editors.

VII

Faerie.
Even the word does not stay still.

Fairye, let me hear

The fluid and formal first words that every mother dreads,
But every poet longs to hear, the child's laugh and ancient cheer,
For novelty new born upon the earth, brewed and boiled
In the grail of an eggshell cup:

"I am as ancient as all the woods of the west,
And all the painted paper in which I am dressed,
But never have I seen or been such a thing before,
Though my lean tongue is tired and my hard heels sore."

Your feet tread on eggshells; their crack is your speech.

VIII

Sometimes, I hear

Far away, and half forgotten,
The music of a humdrum child kept
Beneath a pillared and rising hill.

On the shadowed side of some fayre Sidhe,
A tithe to hell traded for a leaf of laurel lay

Teethes in an inferno's maw.

I know we're not supposed to have favourites, but
I love you more than any weak, wan, womb-born whelp.

IX

Changeling child,

You wear thin; you wear thin pale eggshell skin,
A hefty egg-shaped head, and speckled spriggan skin.

I clothe you in my own flesh;
A babygrow for a baby that will never grow.

I have a father's torn beard, and a mother's suckled breast,
And the papers hate a single parent best.

When I've tossed you into the fires
A little yellow head surfaces, burbles, pops up

From a sizzling egg yolk.

JULEBUKKING

It must terrify you, that words said in a certain way
Can tear you from your house.

Come and wear goatskin with me.

Step with me on the scattered snowflakes;
Pentagram shapes weigh down the white world tonight.

Hooves leave a hard imprint, a dark wet mark.

Hoof-clop like the noise your tongue makes
When it leaves the roof of your mouth.

I leave a goat's head on your porch
Next to the old broom and car windshield scraper.

CRYPTID (THE MYSTERY OF WATER)

the water cascading and churning like a simmering cauldron.
— 'Strange Spectacle on Loch Ness', *Inverness Courier*, 1933

Let me decipher your key.

The neck that curves like the line of beauty
Of the poem I intend to write some-point tomorrow.

The slow wet grace of the snail skin shadow,
The liquid and unheard word of a gainsaid grail.

The water cascading and churning
Like a witch's shimmering cauldron.

The taste of loud slurped primordial soup.
And the smell of the afterburp.

The lock of uncut hair that gets in your face.
And the blur of your finger's quick flick.

A trick of black and white.

The high and demonic denomination
Of a cryptocurrency.

The password that is simply "uncrackable."

When we find the beast, snacking in its nest,
Roll the soft white of our eyes over its ruminant neck,
Drag it to shore and lock it to a shape,

We'll only ask it what weird white fish lives unblinking
Beneath its slime, and, unanswered, toss it back.

ODE TO A MAGPIE / ONE FOR SORROW

O for a beaker full of the warm South
— John Keats, *Ode to a Nightingale*

Keats can keep / his numb tongued nightingale; / I'll save my
stolen silver speech / for my pale and black / kleptomaniac. /
Magpie, your bad luck beak is slick / with Satan's serpent blood
/ and was / silent, / when all the others bayed for Christ / on
his wet-blooded bough. / When Noah took to his Ark, / you
alone stayed, / and strayed / to see the world drown, / to hear
the secret knowledge of its last words, / and drink down its last
/ best / breath; / and like Noah, / swallowed your sorrows, and
became Bacchus's bird, / with wine-dark wings. / When all the
other blackbirds were put in a pie, / you stole the silverware, /
and carved out a bad name for yourself. / The world gives good
mornings / to the one who heard its last good nights, / who would
not shelter, / or sing / for a god on his beam. / Bad luck bird – be
trod upon. / Bridge / the starry silver stream. / Link us / to the
weaver of worlds / and words.

THE CRYING OF THE GULLS

Between the shadow line on sand of your parasol
And the lapped slush beside the salt threshold

Her hunting ground moves
With the light and the tide.

Her dark painted nails dip in the white pool
Of Mr Whippy's spilt beach bleach

Like livid pupils, small in the sick waters
Of her mascaraed eyes.

Sometimes the swaying of the black fans
Around her pink legs catches a man's eye.

But not even the most tremulous twitcher
Looks for long at her yellow lips, marked

By a red beauty spot,
And the long grey bruises of her arms.

The thick muscle of her neck undulates,
Jaw unhinges, and untouched by the waves

Of arms, she lets the slick suntan grease
Ease the passing.

Between the beach's squashed chips and faded newsprint
She plucks and swallows a knotted spotted handkerchief.

EARTH GIANT

Grunged up from the slit hill,
Winches lift him from the cack.

The crisscrossed crane girders bend and strain;
His mouth hangs like a tree bole.

Hacked by looks and hefted sticks,
Soil pours off him in clumps.

Punctured by rods that scrape
Across the henge of his bones

(Stone tinctured in iron),
His moans tremble the quarry.

Men in hi-vis tap and scribble,
Brandish clipboards.

Pointing witches in white hats,
Or plastic knights with new lances.

Floodlights clang on and drown out
The black bubbles of his eyes.

The prepared straps huddle
The square of his shoulders,

The limbs that curve like trunks,
And thicken at root and canopy.

The muddy mallets of his fists
Are yet to pop and splay

The twist and shake of his fingers,
The ore of his cracked nails.

He leaves softer flames, caved in portacabins,
Stumpy footprints in a heaped mound

And men burst like wineskins
As their bodies stretched in his hands.

Whoever they were, it was a querulous
Quest, or a shoddy summoning.

Their villages will worship
The sparse rocks in his lips.

DEAR SYDNEY GRAHAM

Under your blue hat.
— W. S. Graham, *Dear Bryan Wynter*

I

My feet wear odd socks today, one of yours,
One of mine, see how well they go together.

Apologies, I've come to your funeral late,
Dressed oddly and for a night on the town.

II

A pint of foaming seawater with Malcolm Mooney,
Lent out, for a short while, to fast from death and form
A lasting impression. Together
We can moon over whatever midnight moonlit furry
Queens and meropian mermaidens have set aside their fish
Tails and crowns to land in this dive and prop up the bar.

Chat them up with old jokes and new famous phrases;
A dead man makes a fine wingman.

III

Hungover, next morning,
Still hanging on, at the very end of the land,

I go dayfishing.

I go dayfishing, and the ghosts come at night.

And by day I dream

I dream you'll wash up upon the shore, in alien
Whiteness, like some deep sea creature.

But I know, Sydney, you're on the other side of earth.

IV
There is distance
Between us

Like the hard space between
Pen and paper.

V
I linger by the swept shoreline and seven seas,

Unready for the Eighth Journey you go on.

VI
The voice breaks

The still winter seas crack

I hear you

Capped beneath blue braes.

VII

I wear seaweeds and nakedness;
I fold your flotsam into me, like ocean floated origami.
I drink my own salt tears.

Mooney guides the tide in.

VIII

Damp letters wash up next to my bare feet.
The waves have taken their words, but I will be
Careful not to tread on them.

I HAUNT YOU BACK (A PROSE POEM BOOK REVIEW OF *SURGE* BY JAY BERNARD)

Clad in two tragedies / the red tongues squirm / to unobscure the voices crossed out at ~~New Cross~~ / to catch and green and dress / the words fallen / from Grenfell heights. / *Bernard has sifted through the soot and looted the guilty words / etched in black burn marks* – Mark! / The poet comes not with the first responders / feet walk slowly with the burden / of rhyme and trepidation and care / not to disturb the crisp bodies / like Orpheus on a day trip to Pompeii / here to make the stone souls speak. / – Hear! / *A new poet has erupted onto the scene / (of the investigation) / these poems are the smoke that spills / from the cleft mountain lip.*

Inhale the sweet smell of meat / breathe out the sweet sixteen fourteen / the dead languages learned. / They haunt you / you haunt me / I haunt / until we have a legion of ghost children / flyting down Fleet Street / in sheets / that ripple like clear pools disturbed by dreams.

THE TRAIN GOES BACKWARDS

The apparition
— Ezra Pound, *In a Station of the Metro*

Peeled faces look down, don't notice the tunnel;

The dry white ghosts of plants scream against the stopped pane.

THE FIFTH SEASON

When it's so far past midnight
The hands of the doomsday clock

Have fallen off.

When the fifth season, the season that is final
And forever, warms and winters the worn out Earth

We will stand in the sand and glass of the broken
Timepiece and ask it to flow.

THE RITE OF WINTER (A SEQUEL TO *LE SACRE DU PRINTEMPS*)

Part I: The Kiss of the Earth is Rough and Stubbly

After the ritual, the girl claws her way out;
The dead earth crowns.

Her plaited hair tethers her to the split soil
Like some vast umbilical. Snaps with a brace of ice.

Her bones are twisted wire, barbed,
They tug against her skin, compressed,
They coil into

Springs.

Riotous clouds drop torn up notes, scatter snowflakes,
To weigh down the world with pentagram shapes. Her feet are light.

Her feet are bloody from leaping spheres,
Seasons, lifetimes.

No girls surface from the river.
They split their skulls on the icy skin.

Part II: The Sacrificed

Through the mirror she sees who she would have been
Grown old.

Winter's dance is in snap-thaw jerks, her body
Cracks.

The Sage was old even in spring, in winter
She makes him dance dead feet on hot coals.

Often, he treads on his beard, for the boards she trod.

Her lover is dead. Yarilo sleeps and next season
Will take a new bride. Her spirit is suffused

With his spent seed, the last volts of the votive rite.

She leaps; she will never touch the ground again.

THE SIREN STAR

On the first day, in the place empty of it,
The spaceman cracked his nose

Till his visor did the same.

On the second, his grieving replacement,
Sent out to complete the essential maintenance

Downed tools
Unlatched the white umbilic cord.

On the third day, the astronomers with their one wrinkled eyes,
And the children given a telescope for their birthdays

By parents with too much disposable income
And too few ideas, disposed of their sight.

On the fourth day, those who lived in overgrown concrete
Cities snarled and starved of light, unpowered by the spark

Of their own invention, stood in the unshadowed fields
Looking up.

Like a sailor, far from shore, surrounded by nothing
And nowhere, they turn their gaze to the horizon

To see another sight, to burn away the infinite
Fields of grey and green and blue and white.

On the fifth day
There were no seeing men left.

On the sixth, no women.

On the seventh, the last man put on his suit
And left the station

His eyes sealed by the flame from his kitbag.
Even then, he was still called to see.

The citizens of the sun. Three copper women scarred
By the lines of three black holes at their necks

Sucking in starlight.

Three eyeless women, hair and gowns rippling like flags
In an impossible wind.

The ends of hard white limbs clotted black.
Exposed to empty chaos.

She lifts his heavy glass mask
And makes first contact with her lips.

A pursed eclipse of dark-blooded skin bordered in bronze
And the scratch of fingers hard as metal on his Adam's apple.

From that day we took our breaths from blackness.

ODE TO APOLLO 11

We listen here on earth
— John Keats, *Ode to Apollo*

Apollo, you give breath to poets,
And need none yourself;

Far above us, you swallow black.

You fire the arrow made of men and steel and challenge.
Ten times you have drawn the billion dollar bow
And learned from your misses, your Houstonian problems,
That the widows of your flyts burden your godhead.

You dip your arrows in flames and thunder.

As he rose his new-forged armour shone
And dimmed the light of hot Hyperion.

A splash of adamantine shuttle and white starlight
Against the black,

Like an inverted printed page.

Today, you are lighter than ink, and tree skin;
Lighter than breath.

Today, you live in the mouth of your priest.
He has a white body, and a black face;
In his visor's reflection trace the expectant eyes
Of an entire race.

He walks the silver sickle shape,
Reaps the feast of virgin dust and starlight;
Speaks the words the world remembers.

He touches the goddess's skin.
It is dry and wisps away at his step.

Poets' god, you create new worlds,
Walk the dead orb magnificent in desolation.

Apollo, god of poetry, prophecy, and moonboots.

KEEPING WATCH

On the first day of lockdown, I stopped my watch
And hung it on my writing desk.

To slip beneath the wrinkles of Time's face
And sleep within the sandy trench.

I hope I will wake.

I hope I will wake, clamber from my tired bezel,
My sagging gilded case, rise

Like Arthur and sweep the rheumy mist
Of Camlann from my new ancient eyes.

Feel the tickle of my leafy crown, unwilted
By still and silent revolutions.

Touch my startled hand to the thick brush
That covers my face, verdant as the kingdom

My pupils paint, and see the shadow of my graveside
Sundial dialled down to a thin line, hard discerned on stone.

I hope I will wake and find my hands transcribed my dreams
While I slept, my words caught in a willow hoop of ink.

Wake to a collection, two pamphlets, and a fat memoir.

On the first day, I stopped my watch
And hung it on my writing desk.

At permanent twelve.

THE CORONA PRINCE

By now, you must have heard his legends.
You abide in his empire.

In the kingdom of the rising star
He rose from a small bowl of hot bat soup

Pausing long enough for sunken eyes,
Slimed in matted hair, to glare like an alligator

Surfacing to see the prey come to drink.

He stood full height, small feet in the primordial,
A hungry ghost in black scaled armour.

Skin the colour of hardened phlegm.
Consistency of a patagium wing.

The old man's whistle cut short
Before it could cool the broth on his upraised spoon.

With the red light behind him,
The West saw only a body, a thin line of shadow:

A judgement of God over Egypt.
And turned aside their gaze.

On the other side of the sun they say
He fell from the stars with the ink black space

Poured onto the armaments of men
Under the shadow of an eagle's wing.

In truth, his womb is the mucus
Of your lungs the red crown points pierce

As they breach and spit the flesh
As he flails and splutters from the eldritch.

He is born a thousand times each day.
The thin golden string of your life

Is his cut umbilic cord.

His ritual ointments are soap and wine
Darkened water. Courtiers, wring your hands.

His long fingers will squeeze the drops
From your neck, like a tight mink scarf.

For libations, he sups the sweat of his subjects.
Like Stoker's creature he hovers by the bedside

And runs a cracked tongue; stokes flames.

His palaces are spotless white.
With the pomp of pale robes and gurney carriages

He leads procession after procession
Down the scrubbed and stretching corridors.

A pied piper with a liking for liver spots
And time folded into wrinkles.

His subjects shuffle behind.

Like poetry,
He lives on breath and air

And the liquid libations, the flecks that cross
The vermillion border.

Unlike poetry,
He does not survive long on paper.

Smiths and scientists labour
To construct the spear

To spike his groin.

Their designs drawn like a meal made
From a cook book covered in spewed up slops.

The ingredients expert eyes discern
In the detritus at the bottom of your bowl:

A thin and silver shard of his crown
And a scraping of his phlegmatic skin.

A king caught in his coronet.

Count to twenty
And you will name his successor.

THE EXPECTED OCCUPANT

arcing from eave to eave, beyond and above.
— Simon Armitage, *An Unexpected Guest*

Swollen fingers fondle the balustrade, hot
Under the stoaty cloak, skirt out stunted,

Fumble for the coolness of stone,
And from ermine ferret out the cold reason.

His whole life he has waited for death in an ancient place.
The setting of the plates grinds him to dust.

The urn and ash remain a man.
The greyest of men.

Purple in his pantomime pomp; so expensive
It looks cheap, like the bright robes of lords.

Kings and reapers have their robes chosen
For them in life and death. A grim tale.

The bones of his family propped around him like thick
Invitations posed on a mantle, or atrophied antlers, mounted.

A man grows into an odd weak shape, when gold bars
Curb his narrow crib long into an adult hood.

It is the curse of his line that chafing crowns
Bring about baldness and show the skull.

He has waited so long the grin has begun to show
And the carnival below is ready to rob his carcass.

He looks up and waits again for the airshow
In a sky that rebels against headlines of royal blue.

Spies fighter jets, sharp nibs sprung with the quarrel,
And redder birds spat out, caught in the infernal machinery:

The bent beam's bloody spoil.

The roar of the little lions below mewls
Lighter now the bowmen are gone.

The tight grief kept unspoken at the back of his throat
Like centuries of uncoughed phlegm.

The chains he has dangled on his pierced tongue
Constrict, with all the charm of gardened snakes.

The long serpents have swallowed all the spiders,
Deprived his fingers of the exercise of trapping them.

His wife wears insects. The jets leave a trail of pesticide.
He waves his hand, feeble fronds to fan before a pharaoh.

If he was closer, perhaps he'd peep the bent back
Of a pink old woman, as much blood in her as him.

We have taken off our black hats, and go bare of wreaths
Or tight skull belts.

Let the scriptured weeds grow, without stricture
Or knowledge of the shape of crowns

Or protectorate.

Yes, arcing green over gold, from leaf
To leaf, before and again.

Republican laureates
Breaking lines.

SUNDOG HOWL

Better bring / a shovel.
— Scott Walker, *Sundog*

When Scott Walker died he left me his voice,
Tore out the redness of his throat and pressed it in black.

Scott, you go night flying
And I walk in the day.

I put my ear to your coffin.
Heard nothing.

You promised you'd be listening,
You and Brel; bet you're getting along real well.

They buried you like a dog's bone
Finished playing.

Scott, you walk beneath the earth.
There's no dancing near your grave.

The later stuff, you couldn't dance to.
Thought I'd bring a shovel, and a show.

Later, I heard you punching the meat
Over by the funeral spread.

The thumbs of spring
Have soused your eyes.

The disc turns and turns again.

The sundog sets
The sundog plays
Another set piece.

PHILIP PULLMAN'S GRADUATION
In hat of antique shape, and cloak of grey
— Matthew Arnold, *The Scholar-Gipsy*

I

I keep your life's work on the bottom shelf
Next to the snarled cluster of electrical wires
So it may gather dust. So it may gather dust,

When I forget to polish, or the demon at my shoulder nips at me,
Like a suit of thin white armour, that nags me with quick paper
cuts,
And this world and its trivialities and the reality of its upkeep falls
away.

These are the words hard discerned in dust.
The hairs on the back of my hands have fallen
And mingled in the stuff, these hands I have made
Into brushes – push their own bristles about.

So I can see the invisible, you could not disguise
It from a poet, the wit of your dust Pan pun.

II

You see the waking spires like Dante
Saw the red slate topped rooves.

Like Florence and its Dante, you will never possess this city,
But one day it will possess you, your image subtle cut from marble
And blazed loudly on china mugs and expensive tea towels.

There could never be Philip's Oxford,
Like there is a Lyra's Oxford, red bound, neat,
Definitive. There are too many thrown hats in the air
And voices raised in dissent. But I think you will like that.

A city is a soul that lives on after death.

III

I know you do not believe in a life after death,
So I am writing to you now.

They should bury you in a cathedral (for its dreaming tower),
And because you always were an atheist inhabiting a vast religious
edifice,
A republican, with noble heirs of grey and gold falling from his
crown.

When you are banished by some darker robed Black Guelph,
Cante dei Gabrielli di Gubbio with a skinless skull face,

Death will come, like the ripple of black cloth
Stretched taut over a square frame
And the roar of mortars in the air.

Flung, like a marionette with cut wire strings.

IV

Pip, I pull and spit the seeds from my teeth, blow
The grey cloud from your low-shelved soul's armour.

You have given us your paradise that slips
With every moment it stays in our hands
Like a fine peeled apple, but know this:

When from the other world the ephemera of your comedy,
Some playbill scrap of some celebrated adaptation,
Is tossed, wind-borne, through a fresh cut slit –
It will flail and catch on my shiny black shoes.

MAGPIE'S BIRDBATH

And Crow yawned – long ago
He had picked that skull empty.
— Ted Hughes, *The Battle of Osfrontalis*

He wants nothing.

There is a deep calm, a still and silent birdbath
In an overgrown and empty courtyard
The flock has not found. He fills his small black breast.

The vines shade the gentle light. Lichen covers the stone wall.
The forest waits through the cracks. It will wait a little longer.

Beak furrows the water. Wing nestles the small stone lady,
Some siren or sea nymph, water spooling from her open mouth.

The turquoise streak says you are of the pool, it is of you.
Head moves in stop motion from one instance to the next.

He swallows and baptises his throat.
Makes the staggered cry like Sellotape stretched out.

Looks down through clear liquid and sees the stone bottom.

He lines his days with silver.

WINTER

Thus, though we cannot make our Sun
Stand still, yet we will make him run.
— Andrew Marvell, *To His Coy Mistress*

But night is long.

It stretches like a ship's mast in darkness
To some height you cannot fathom

With the infinite noise of waves beneath your feet
And the weak boards you have nailed between.

We cannot freeze the sun, but shut your eyes
And you will always have the night.

THE GOBLIN
At the end of the ritual
— Ted Hughes, *Finale*

When the human hand closes over the last wavering flame
An eyeless and pellucid worm squirms in the dark.

When nothing you can see exists
The atomic empires throw electronic war.

When the earth cracks at last molten men drip forth
And bleed their life force over the dry earth.

When the tsunami hits
He takes out a straw.

When the beard of a god and oceans have wisped away
A long white and aberrant bristle sprouts from his cheek.

When the last holy book is shut or burnt for smoke
He sluices himself large on the cave wall.

When the four end and the fifth season, that is all, begins,
His fingers steeple the globe, jab sinkholes, spin hurricanes,
Squeeze hot floods, bring heat and cold with the movements
Of his blood, and his nails scrape furrows for the beasts to work.

When you have heard it all,
The goblin scratches a pick on the curls of his teeth.

THE LESSER GOD PAN

Non-stick coating
Tangled in the earth.

The snare holds your handle
Your handle levers the earth.

Blackening.

You have outlived ancients.

With a prang
A hoof steps onto the black plate.

EPIMETHEUS ON HIS CRAG

in the end, with the heaven-sent girl.
— Ted Hughes, *Prometheus on His Crag*

Sodden underfoot the flooded marsh at last
Meets the rock shaped like a shout of frozen flame.

He has outlived his brother
Who outlived the vulture
Who swallowed the sun;

There are dark marks about his eyes.
He has been drinking. Only a trickle.

Crowned with the human gift, a hind:
A stag of antenna, an old sock, a wind chime.

Only a jangle of ephemera.

She pads to an old washed up fridge box
Door hanging rust-scorched from its hinges.

There is no hum like the soft bodies of bees meeting.

Her soft nose nuzzles his side
Her paraphernalia slices an ancient liver spot.

Cuts skin like a box-cutter.

A PROSE POEM BOOK REVIEW OF TERRANCE HAYES'S *AMERICAN SONNETS FOR MY PAST AND FUTURE ASSASSIN*

> *fire with my two tongues / Loose*
> — Terrance Hayes, *American Sonnet for My Past and Future Assassin*

You say even the odour of your breath / can be assassinated (p. 17). I have stuck my nose in / and tried to reconstruct / the meal you ate before you perished. / Maybe I put a bit too much / daylight in with the twilight, / skimmed the milk, / and got vaped instead of smoked. / (See again / page 17).

Most of the shape of the meat / and the bones that lived beneath / are gone; / but the cloak keeps the overall outline / bent by centuries of use. / *Hayes poses and counter-poses / his jambalaya and the jumbled ire / of his assassin / within the limits of his form. / Hayes melts down Petrarch's pedestal and petrified edifice / and leans down on the wet clay.* / The bronze lady melted down / in her own green flame / and distilled into swaying scaffolds; / *Hayes relaxes on the loose metal hammock / he has made. / His voltas dimly charged or discerned, / silent hinges that don't squeak like the old ones, / at least not always so loud: 'almost / Unhinged lyrics' (p. 41).*[1] / Some sniff. / You can call these poems sonnets / like you can call that big electric fence / a wall / Shakespeare / Petrarch / AWOL.

The quick and quirk / of ampersands amplify the casual, / sand down your lines / *denote the poet's drafting process in the work*

---

1.   FOOTNOTE. / All references waddled from the Penguin edition / pop culture / Shop Road culture / high culture / rope round the neck / and drop / low culture / and other poetic vultures. / Note the rhythm of his feet / as he dances / and holds his face / p. 18.

itself, / typographic marks / to mark the urgency of his sonnets ¦ and subjects. / As you yourself would no doubt acknowledge / a bullet is still quicker / & stills quicker, / than even a poet on fire / under fire / on a two poems a day streak / of soot and finger smoke.

The repetitions of the title reproduce the cyclical histories / indicated in the title. The repetitions of the title / pay homage to Wanda Coleman, / homes the words in American soil. / It reads like a refrain. Buries you / in American earth / and locks you / in a sonnet music box. / You are not a prophet when you say 'when a knee or shoe stalls against his neck' (p. 77). / You are just state-ing a past that is sure to unite with future tense, / like <u>there will be another poem.</u> / *Hayes ends his sonnet 'Rilke ends his sonnet...' saying 'Define life' (p. 37).* / Hayes ends his sonnet seventy times. / Seven times more / and maybe we can forgive him this.

The poems are expansive / – the pages inexpensive (I paid / £9.99 for mine) – / figure out such figures as: / Plath and Hughes / (no, not that one), / Davis & Hendrix, / Baldwin & Dickinson, / Coltrane & Coleman, / Morrison, / Aeneas, Odysseus, / your father, Our Father, / a father searching for two sisters / to broaden their lips with God's name, / Jesus & His sister, / the rhythmed and unrhythmed / reflecting on how to dance. / *Similarly expansive is the apostrophic 'You'. / You are the reader, / the assassin, / the United States citizen, / the poet in residence / in Langston's love chamber, / a prisoner, / a listener, / a sexual confidante, / America / & the American president.*

You mention 'Dr. Who' (p. 77) / in passing / like the hero visiting / the world of the week and weak / and you say a sonnet is a bird

in a dark box, / perhaps, you should have said / if The Donald
dumped a sonnet / – hate shouted through an office shaped
megaphone trumpet – / it would be like a Dalek in its trash can /
firing laser bolts at random. / Seemed like a missed opportunity.
/ Historically / they've both had problems with stairs. / Stare / at
the shine / *of Hayes's unglossed heteroglossic text.* / Hayes is a Time
Lord / lauded for the time taken to sonnet / in the time lard was
a president / greased resident in the White House. / At least the
eagle / had the dignity to admit it was bald.

Add to all this lonely heart ads. / Critic seeks poet / who can sum
up 13 unlucky red and white lines in a fourteen line form / or at
least dazzle him with starlight / enough so he can wrap his eyes in
cloth / and forget about looking. / Here's the hook: / a critic can
be an assassin to a book. A critic is your 'mother's [...] shadow'
(p. 65) / watching over you / telling you what to do / what not to
do / sometimes bewildered / but trying hard to understand. / A
critic wears half 'his boy's face', / and like the father of pee dot 43,
/ tries to see out of an eye / with an X and a different sex in it.

I'll give you five / if you'll give me fifty.
I give you five / you give me fifty.

You don't need my garlands. / The body of page 17 / was swiftly
found / (on page 17) / and identified as you / and heaped with
flowers. / The thorns we found / doled out / to prick a twenty
foot baby balloon. / If we stand on each other's shoulders / if we
make a pyramid (absent the gold and gaud of his mock-Egyptian
tower / – he crammed the rectangle block / into the triangle
shape / of a child's IQ test / he didn't cram for), / we can let the
air out / the old wind / in an orange flesh box.

Your voice is so strong in these poems, / I knew what you wculd sound like / before I ever heard you speak / though, I'll admit, / I wasn't expecting you to sing one / in the literal and not just the literary sense / the time I heard you read, / Newcastle, / Twenty-Nineteen. / *Hayes blurs and fogs / the divisions / between music and page work. / Hayes preserves the conventional verbal cues of the sonnet, / those 'Ohs!' and 'Ahs!' updated to: / 'Whatever. I'm just saying' / (p. 18). /* At the penultimate / *he is 'almost grown tired of talking to you.'*

When you die the mourner-poets will gather / every one of them eager with a golden shovel / and fingers itching with the Midas touch. / Heavyheads / gather with grief and intellectual / pronoun-cements / a-straining / ascertaining / arse-sing / the mus-cells of their music to coin The New Famous Phrase. / Sometimes, as with Dalí / it will take ten years / (page / eighty- / two). / Dirty danglers dig / while the dirt & the seeds and the flowers talk / dirty / and the assassin cocks. / 14 rounds / ready to go / in the chamber.

If I said it right today / I lorded under time / and said it long before.

Line your coat with these words. / *On the day the assassin comes / this is just the slim volume / to stop the bullet /* and leave breath's black burn marks / across the metal skin.

This is just the outline in chalk / of the corpse of the assassinated. / Step over the border line / and the body will find you. / Poet, your pages are printed on white paper, / but when I pick up / your collection / it's like being given my / green / card.

LADY OF THE ROCK

A piece of moon splashed into the sea.
And on it, the citizens of a white and dusty empire.

As soon as their feet touched where the silt
Met the waves, their bodies began to twist.

The kicking legs of the first drawn together
And fused and scaled and sealed; she howled at her transformation.

The shine of the second's midnight hair
Untouched by earth's gravity, rippling like the shoalmated

Became snakes and bit her skin pink, till quieted
By a few lines of chosen song.

The third was the one I loved, hazel feathers
And yellow eyes, black pupils a serifed line.

The dark strokes of her eyes a shadowed doorway
To other worlds. A place to be born from.

They recline in their pockmarked castle,
Preach of beauty from their barnacled pulpit.
Guard the sea-salt grail.

How many men have drowned in these holy waters,
Smashed against this rock, this church?

From the prow, arm outstretched I hold aloft the sigil
Of a thin string, beads and a wooden cross.

A small raft to cling to.
And pray that when I step out

I will walk across the waters.

TWICE THE MAN

stare / in a mirror long enough and he would come.
— Gregory Leadbetter, *Mirror Trick*

Under cover of the sound of sky, the neophytes gather
Where stone is coldest and the forest sleeps.

They bring out the long bowl.
They dollop bull's blood in pools at either end.
They breathe onto the mirror pane.

An old headmaster, the lines of shadow under his eyes
Like the subtle curl of a feather's black rachis,
Whose subject has fallen from the curriculum
Like his god from his kingdom, says the words,
Weighs out the Greek gramarye on his tongue.

Then they all look up.

They look up so long
Their age begins to tell.
There is not a Greek among them.

When the frayed bolt hits He is for a moment infinite.
He is for a moment infinite, in a way a man can be infinite,
Not in a womanly shape of eight asleep,
But in a single line stretching like a pillar
Glistering through earth and sky,
Time become a single number counting up in blue digital light,
Like a single sentence without a full stop,
A poetry that for all its complexity

And unbroken lineation cannot be understood.
He finds the hot forge at the core;
He puts on the lightning crown.
The thorn crown blinks, Allah winks out,
The countless Hindu deities go uncounted,
Sikh sheaths go empty and unsought, turbans unspool,
The circumcised go uncircumcised,
Budai's swollen belly is vexed and goes concave,
And highest throned Nothingness is filled.

All the holy books go blank and blue.

The raised eyebrows of the men disappear.
Clouds fill their heads. Too dark, too bright.

Shards split and catch the blue webs of their palms.

Jove, one cries, *Zeus*, spits the man, *Dyaus*;
They fight, and in the confusion another man dies.
Seared retinas flash with hot snapped silver knives
That show insides their insides.

The mirror goes black and cracks.
Light retreats into the high roiling depths.
The blade sticks in the head.

Steel is better than iron better than
Bronze better than lead.
But in a pinch an empty shine will do.

The men look for eagles. None.
After three hours the men mizzle off.

It is raining, and there are no birds.
It is a long slipping march back to the city.

Shiva starts counting enemies.
Christ's forehead begins to bleed,
Mecca turns men like a compass point,
Hands find hilts, heads are covered,
A stomach swells with warm and worshipful breath,
And all else is reversed and forgotten.

They should have waited nine.

The blade becomes a babe with reflective skin;
The embrace is never fruitless.

She climbs out of the dark sticky body.
On her flesh, Athena shows the clouds.

The daggers of her teeth curve with her thoughts;
The father outwitted – no, inwitted – by the daughter.

Out of any, he wore an old shape too long;
When the altars emptied his death came all the quicker.

DEATH BY EARTH
the stages of his age and youth
— T. S. Eliot, *Death by Water*

They stand like tall darkhouses. Belt buckles on their hats,
Like their heads were waists. Straining against the gristle
They have grown fat on. They dragged her ashore, fishtail flailing.

Tall hats, rough hands, black clothes and wire nets.
Her mouth shaped in red despair. Handful after handful of dust
Until she could no longer read their palm lines.

They swallowed her in wet clay
Like a man drowned a foot from the shore.

Scoured her with scooped handfuls of dust.

The sea, the sea, damn the sea. The seabirds cried for their helping
And the waves retreated. My heartscales squirm and shake for
vengeance.

A death as ugly as the rock. Above her they build the sandy road.
I could spend a lifetime searching for those harmed dried bones
To swallow or hang about my neck.

STEPS TO ENGRAVEN THE EARTH (A PROSE POEM BOOK REVIEW OF JO CLEMENT'S *MOVEABLE TYPE*)

The horse's eye like a dark brown lake. / Ah, I see, the first verse page is a pool. / Sparkling / self-reflective / the poems ahead, golden apples, / glinting / at the bottom of the waters, / like the red strike that lines the equine iris. / Apples fallen in a cornea field.

White straw mane curves down onto black horse flesh / like the ink and white of the engraver's art. / *Clement has curled the wood shavings from the block / compacted lines flow with the grain.* / Bewick's candle wick flames down and Clement's licks up, / and then exchanged, / like leaping fountains, but of flame.

Like the wood block dipped in paint and pressed to the page / Clement holds you to it.

My favourite lines: 'admit to the skim / of blood that can't settle', / the eyes catch on / no reader could skim past. / *Sometimes / the poems operate in pairs.* / Ironwork and Smithsong are the shoed and sleeved hooves of two women / acting a pantomime horse / sealed / with metal wire cross stitches. / Or land hard and tie themselves to you: 'bound hooves in hessian and hay to flit town / in the dead of night, wraithing cobbles to keep quiet'; / silence you / like a magician / drawing the unexpected card.

At Appleby Fair / fair words fall like ripe apples / with gravity / and discovery. / Dip / in Eden River, / apple bobbing / in the preservative of Clement's slick cranial fluids. / She has brought us to the waters / and she has made us drink.

Listen to the hoof clop / the sound her tongue makes / when it leaves the roof of your mouth. / Don't overlook / the won whinny and snort / of this gift horse's shout. / Poet, / thank you / for letting us travel with you.

THE MAGI'S CAMEL

With the voices singing in our ears
— T. S. Eliot, *Journey of the Magi*

The fat god squats between back braes.

Does not discern the soft gasp as hoof meets grit;
Even the dust fears the determined, unerring hammer

Of two dark nails.

The murmur of cloth, creaking leather and dry lips,
The gold of a weak winter's sun, a thin wash for a parched place.
The sense behind, of a conversation on direction spoken frank.

This is a life with few gifts; noses closed to scent,
Thick lashes shading even the season's poor wealth.
The murder of your bones by flights of carrion birds.

The shaggy and silken fortress moves,
Gains and loses territory with every step.
Stamps the sand with an alien sigil.

A creature with six hands; two to bear the whip,
Four to do the work. The adoration of the magi is a tough love.

The way always, of those of the hill
And those who speak from the mount.

Slick guts work the miracle;
A drop will last a week.

A drink lasts longest for those last to drink.

Only the sight of a horse without rider, white and old as starlight,
Running masterless among long grasses, cooled and stilled by night,
Stirs the hard muscle of a young heart from its dry and steady beat.

The blurred and furry pulpit makes its way across the desert.
Magicians preach from the turret, but none here will follow the hard way.
For all they say, only thick soles and spindle limbs know the hardness.

They know the weight of all the far travelled books of sorcery.
The washerwomen and shepherds jeer, fling earth;
They have their own magic to work.

Yes, three kings, three trees, a star, a child,
But two humps.

Discarded crowns gain swift burial in the desert.
No, the way back the same as the way there.

THE SEA CHAIN
After H.D.'s Oread

The anchor string stretches
From inches below her nipple

Over blue braes, hurled green pines
And down my throat.

Hazel feathers shake. Strong arms tremble.
Talons on rock. Feet on wood.

SIREN'S THROAT

Deep in the cave of your ear
— Ted Hughes, *The Minotaur*

Beneath the verdant top where she roosts
There is a maze of aeolian catacombs.

Lined with strings, the walls shake with her songs.
Her breath is felt even at the cave lip.

Despite her feathers,
I do not say this as the hen-pecked husband:

She knows everything, she tells less.

I say it as a suitor, first foot ashore.
Leather boot leaves a hard imprint on the coast.

I have seen flowers grow from sand
In the furrows of her claws.

I have seen invertebrate sea beasts scuttle
And crack the chitin of their shells in her wake.

The stone as pale and white as doves and Dover;
I am far from home.

I warm my hands on the chalky rock
And tear up my maps.

In her Throat I hear the echoes of her lips,
The crunch of apple, and the laughter of her sisters.

When she spares me a thought,
Fruit tumbles and catches in the nooks.

I tie a golden thread to my chest hair,
Crack no more nails on the ascent.

When the next prow splits the shore,
I will be her minotaur.

A GUIDE TO THE STONES (FOR CASTLERIGG)

the mimic arrangement of stones
— William Wordsworth, *Guide to the Lakes*

Children scuffle for the seat, sit, and depart
When the war moves on, and I find my place.

More leaning than relaxing, a sarcastic courtier,
Joking over the infant tyrants throned on stone.

As a mere's mirror, man's small mountains, chiselled rock
Against a backdrop too large for any hammer.

But others are talking too, of sandwiches and ice creams,
Of the slow walk back, or car seats and difficult straps,
And the easeful storm drowns a druid's quiet thunder.

A castle rigged against invasion
By the space between the stones.

ANEIRIN

Gochorai brain du ar fur caer
Cyn ni bai ef Arthur.
   — *Y Gododdin*

Aneirin, an air in furs let into a lordly place.
He staggers in with the wind.

Slips, and skins his palms and knees on the stones.
The last legend of a year-long pub crawl
Makes his entrance; moves from foot level to table,
Slides into the poet's trance.

The blue armour of his grieving stance:
Full height, eyes roving, feet still, a drink
Where his shook hands can reach.

Aneirin's skin is glass; in hall they see distorted
The stretched faces of the men behind him.

The froth and foam of a shake of the horse's lips
Settles a scum on a small gold lake.

Tongue forever slick with the wet of mead,
Loud and confident as a man drunk, he mourns.

Though he was no Arthur
Hands reached for him from the glass.

The hands hardy, burly, lordly, friendly,
Not the thin cold white of some unearthly lady.

He wore the bee's blood lather best and slid
Between the din, the trampling of men under iron-shoed
Men and the high screams of the horses.

His skin dappled in the white hives of the fearful,
His armour striped, yellow-black.

The taste of blood salt and mead sweet;
The vapour from his mouth plumes like the hovering souls.

If he were to give one more drop for each man
His mouth would go dry, his skin peel invisible.

He is a skilled barman; knows just how much to pour.
He flicks a settled fuzzy bug from the curving rim.

Only when he is done do they empty their glasses;
The drinking solution to all his problems.

Ravens pick at killed men and living insects.
The poet lives a honeyed life.

Squashed beneath the palm,
You find the dead insect smeared on goat hide.

THE FOOTMAN.

Advertisement
For and after, first, Thomas Gray's 'The Bard. A Pindaric Ode', and second,
John Martin's 'The Bard', Laing Art Gallery, hung under an obsequity to
Edward, who watches from the higher rafters; we present a third instalment.

I.1

Later than dust, he hoicks his tabard,
Spills his drink and kicks his tent, fumbles after.

Tracing the scooped earth and prints, schtum by the stream,
He winces and wets his lips and stubbled neck, dribbles

On thin lions winding down from tail to paw like troop
And wagon flagging on the hard mountain pass.

I.2

Overnight, the technicolour river has smoothed
The skull, its progress scouring flesh and brainpan,

Bleaching weedy strands whiter than the wintry crown.
The summit's plummet has added and taken away, its fruit:

A ruined face outcrops from the rock, the mountain in miniature,
Bouldered by an impacted comet – a neck blistered with a second head.

I.3

By spell or mishap, he reads the splashed runes
Mid-slurp, once, twice, and again, the third.

The fronds of the smashed harp sway and beckon,
But it is the triple-jointed hands that take him under.

Gripped at the vulnerability of his ankle, beneath fall and thunder,
The drenched lions of his coat scrape, claw, and vomit blue.

II.1

The giant's bones are twice his frame.
Sable hollows drink, and need no sight or breath.

They grapple left, they churn right,
Both fighters go gurning forwards and grasping under.

Yes, the giant's bones are twice his frame,
But without muscle, or the new invented sins of sinew.

II.2

Downriver, the web of bardic entrails catch
Fish scales in the elastic of encomiastic guts.

Three eagles observe, crouch, and strut their talons,
Clack fingernails on the warped stones, moult feathers.

At the spirit level and below
Men and denizen tangle in the bed.

II.3

At the limits of his breath, he throws the bones
And his flail hits upon the axe of a missing chin.

Fingers furl, hands feel out the handle, seize a victory
Like the upthrust silken waxen skin of Arthur's selkie.

Three strikes score and key the skeleton, like a scratched car.
The carrion leave without gristle.

III.1

They wash up filthy from the dredge, oiled in the man's salt,
Clothes rent from the torrent; he gathers the rags white as surf

And the bard's toiled body. He starts with the spine and helmet,
Then by weave and lash affixes the spindles of arms and legs to back.

The treeline is further than the shoreline,
But now there is no risk of drowning.

III.2

The cats have fled, but the mountain has not bowed.
And how high an Englishman could climb with eight limbs instead of four,

Spidered on the mountainside, an ink blob on snow.
He will bring these human parts higher than the rounded ramparts.

The king's road is behind. He has been spun to face the mountain's foot.
The king's name makes for a poor ward and catspaw.

III.3

Yes, this foot will make a decent pick
For the ascent – he'll wear your bones,

Compress his breath, loan your ribs for armour.
At the peak there is a stony seat.

"For now, I will stand in the shallows
And suck the marrow from his jawbone."

Milton said the right hand is for poetry, and the left for prose. /
Well, today I'm feeling ambidextrous. / This is a drink that goes
down the wrong way, and the right. / And leaves you spluttering.
/ A two headed magpie, pecking / at its bone-bonded brother, /
stealing its own silver. / Ruffling feathers. / This is Siamese twins
sitting smug in an exam hall. / They've both revised / different
parts. / Two hands pick and tear at each other's finer parts. /
Beneath the nails of one / the blood and dirt of the other. / This
is like reading your palm lines, left hand to right, / and finding
they join up. Like / one page's words, printed over two. / This is
a crossbreed. A turtle sewn to a hare. / All legs on the ground. /
A crossword line. / That can be read up or down. / Two hands
play rock, paper, scissors. / Both choose paper / every time. /
Start playing slaps. One hand bruises the other. / Either way.
Only one person feels the sting. / Two tongues twist beneath my
lips. / Poke from my mouth, split and snakelike. / Twice gifted
chiromancer. / You see farther than a blind bard ever could. /
Write your future with both hands.

A BANQUET FOR PENELOPE
After Ovid's Heroides, I: Penelope to Ulysses

I

Dear visitors, how long was your journey?
How delicious for delicate limbs to twist and ache.

I'm sorry it's dark, you'll have to light it yourself.
I'll wait. He has a match. Thanks for the drink.

There's no ash from asphodel meadows on your boots,
So you must have walked the road some Roman put there,

His father's eyes on the tremble of his back,
And his son's feet stepping out before him

Until they are marching over him, making
Pavement of his bones and tombstone.

II

Every day, I sit and look out over the stream. Dead with thirst,
Parched as ancient parchment, but it's not a wine we can drink.

There's no salt in it,
But I wouldn't call it fresh,

If you filled your careful cup with its froth,
It would end your carefree drinking days,

Though your nights would go on and on.
There are the shapes of sphinxes in the waters;

The riddle my husband sought to answer
By oar stroke and seasickness.

I'm the one who sits by the shore now.
It's the brightest place.

If Hero lay on the other side, not even Leander could swim it,
Though all heroes cross it, one-way only, mostly, of course.

Sometimes chill Achilles meanders by,
Dunking his pale ankle in meagre shallows.

III

Your clothes are strange, but they suit you.
And here's me, cold, in the wisp that I wore

To cheer thirsty young men that are dry
And old ghosts now.

Time is a slow Proteus, and death a quicker one, sooner
Or later we all change our shape, or lose it altogether.

The mechanic tick of its metamorphosis like the slap
Of a tongue leaving the roof of its mouth.

You should have seen how they ate.
Men are pigs. Ask my husband.

Not one of them noticing they were eating us
Out of house and home, king and country.

Men are blind. Ask my husband
About the cyclops and the big pointy stick.

A son sees though; my boy, my buoyant
Telemachus telling the unsuitable

There's wine and girls and tales and a fire outside, masking
The stillness of his hatred by the movement of bronze light.

Luring the indoor men out, like Pan loping naked and goat-legged
With his lips to his pipe to smoke them out to dance.

IV
Receiving you in this hall of Hades and shades
Is like getting a letter from the living world.

You don't even have to say anything.
You can learn a lot from the envelope.

You're all stamped with the same famous faces
That I drank with, lived with, threaded, severed, and delivered.

Did you yield to those forgetful waters, the furrows on your face
Disappearing like a ship's wake, traced a moment on the ocean?

Lethe works like my hands, those nights spent bent over
At the loom, fighting the droop of eyes and the gloom.

I'll rosy my fingers in your wine, and perhaps
I may touch you.

My husband dug a trench as long as his arms
In his day, he was too long at soldiering, silly man.

All that wasted lamb and white barley;
An animal will hardly keep us talking.

Women wait longer than a moon for blood
In this starless, sunless space, where death piles on death.

V

If you look up, you can see the roots of our bedpost,
Though the tree is cut down, the stump stays and the roots grow

Like our tale with every telling. Slice into it and you will see
The long years of our separation written on those rings:

The oh of a siren's lips, yes, and the widening pupil of a cyclops's eye
Learning the name of a flame, the shadowed cave mouth after

The boulder has been rolled away, and the king come out.
The empty circlet waiting for the wisdom of your brow beneath it,

The bright eyes of the owlet wiling away its infinite nights,
Witness to the finesse and fitness of your night attacks,

The sucking circle pit of a monster's whirlpool,
The snapping lips of lithe necks, waiting to swallow you,

The brim of a sorceress's frothing cauldron, and a hat of disguise.
An empty dog's bowl. The arrow's path between axe-heads.

A son, the spitting image, fighting his far-off father's battles for him,
A plate full to the brim and then splat the fat of a dead man's face in it.

Your wife pacing, and circling the bedroom,
Tending the olive branches, and not surrendering.

The ring composition circling our lives
Like the dark shape of scavengers in the sky.

VI

You're probably wondering where he's wandered off to.
You'll see Ulysses, that sunken star, where he always was.

Even in Elysium wounds still weep,
And my husband nurses a boyhood scar.

The tusk of a boar to his boasting foot
Took him away from climbing rocks

And shattering sticks against sticks
And plate armour from the dining hall

And the laughter of his playmates.
They still came to the foot of his sickbed,

That's where he learned to tell his stories;
A wily child, whiling away his childish days.

And now what he saps from his deathbed visitors,
He uses to gather wood from the roots, and bind it together.

A fume drunk on the spirit of flesh,
Hands disguised as the artful living.

The first blood a man gets and he uses it for wood.
Those suitors were all the same. Men.

If you listen, you may hear the far away creak of the boards,
The sails unfurled like bedsheets, the straining of tackle,

The spitting and swearing of the bump of his boat
Against the rusty ferry, forestalling the passage of the dead.

He let me name his raft: *Ithaca*, so he's always at home.
I let him name my son, though I'd say I called the boy down

For breakfast more than he prayed, fatherly, before he slept
On his high-minded mission, to dawdle his fruit on his knee.

He never takes me with him. Perhaps a Penelope cruise
Would be too much woman for him.

He loves that little boat, he swears by the very waters
He'll never see it break. Sometimes, slaked, I help him sew

The slack threads that come undone, that tangle in the weeds,
Like seaweed in the hair of a half-made mermaid.

There's no sirens here to tempt a man;
It is a place without birds.

Any one of us ghosts could walk the waters
And not crack the wineskin.

VII

I'd write still as I did then, but the pen elopes with the hands.
How many of my sweet nothings ended up open and undelivered,

Pillows for lonely, salted sailors, sprayed with my incense,
Dampened, and torn with my tears, and the lengthening years.

Your light's going out, and I think I can hear
The returning ship.

Men are late, and a woman will wait
To have words with them.

The blood has dried on the dust of my lips.
You'll be leaving me now,

Back through the cave and the crust.
We'll meet again, when you too are dust.

Sincerely, don't hurry back.

LIONESS AND PORTCULLIS

Some gave them plum cake / and drummed them out of town.
— *The Lion and the Unicorn*
The world rolls under the long thrust of his heel.
— Ted Hughes, *The Jaguar*

The insignia of her paw rests heavy on the iron gate.

On the other side, the men fail to recognise
The semiotics of her heraldry.

This is a metal she cannot break
With the gnawing of time or teeth.

Eyes nestled in their natural mascara, like suns inhabiting night,
She tracks the movements through the squares.

She has watched this metal made into drum and candle sticks.
She has watched it made into ships, rings, crowns, and irons,
And the very axes to break them. She has seen shelves for women
And men to live in, lampposts, lanterns, and claw-like shivs in the dark,
Wardrobe hinges, engines, and sceptres to knock on the wooden doors
Of parliaments. Bent into edifices on which to hang your whole flesh,
Black crosses become corrugated skeletons that squeak and sting
Her teeth at the thought of a contact to burst her empty belly.

She has spent centuries tortured by the scent without taste;
Some nights she huddles against the cold iron to catch our heat.
By storms she flops her tongue between the bars to smack her lips
With the taste of our tart rain. Is it the long memory of centuries,
Or does the water fizz, no longer as still as in her days of sprawl,
By lakesides, rivers, beaches, and the breaking waters of women?

The wet hairs of her chin drizzle a puddle on our flagstones.
She longs for the rampant challenge: flung fur and paws against bars.

Sometimes she sees him through the grate.
She tracks him now, like prey.

She suspects he has devoured their cubs.
Though her mate may not remember the demigods of her womb
She scents it on his breath when he shouts and the hot cannons'
Hurting and the swords swiped across air wail with him.

Sometimes he walks on two legs and totters like a man,
Kingly eyes hung in a brown mane, yellow fur dimmed.

In this shape, his lion lips are sewn shut. Her eyes shed angered tears
Like the corpse light of the long death of constellations reaching earth.

She hisses as he offers the red jellied delights
Of his flesh like he is prey. Lets them huddle
In his hair like his own sons and daughters.

Sometimes she sees him rest his full fur boots
On a lionskin rug like a golden cloud.

Even when he is not there, in the narrow field
Afforded to her sight, she sees his pawprints
On steel and vertical glass, same as they signed
The quick flat savannahs of their illiterate youth.

Sometimes he goes daubed and peeling in his white and red
Warrior's paint, to play with some other tribe or animal cult,
Dressed like a bleeding ghost.

Her fur ripples like a lone banner in wind.
Her shoulders undulate like swaying tentpoles
In the hands of unsteady men.

An arm reaches through the grate; a gift like a unicorn's horn.
Fingers curl tight around her fur.

Yes, there are gates of fine bone ivory, gates of horn,
And both are hard like metal between teeth, but dreams of flesh
Can fill a low trough groove dug by long prowling.

THE FIRST MAN
After John C. Dollman's Study for 'The Unknown', Laing Art Gallery

Fire streaks like a tear on the page.

A face darker and brighter than ours lives in the vapours.
I fear to trip on the wrinkles and land insubstantial.

On her knees she is taller than my tribe.
Like an obelisk of our stacked expressions.

I think about knocking the apish wig
From her head with the burning branch.

Tearing her tiger's fur from her curves,
Showing the pit from where she has so lately whitely wormed.

She is the first right angle, her pose, a correction
To the careless roughness we have lived in.

To the bending of trees and the outcropping of stones.
To the thrawn timidity of our posture.

I leave, and am not left behind for lameness,
Or sickness, or sameness.

I balance on my hands so my feet
Do not touch the dirt.

Her hand was not pointed at me.

But I feel the curled wishing paws of the others
Jabbing the way at my back.

The days of my exile
Outnumber my toes and fingers.

My hair falls in clumps,
And I learn to shiver.

I cannot eat but for the thought
Of dragging the carcass back to crisp.

I knuckle my mouth:
"It-is-not-good-for-man-to-be-alone."

I know now what she summoned:
She has summoned me.

THE LAST ANIMAL

I will not live among the wild scenes of nature
— Mary Shelley, *The Last Man*

When all the other animals are dead
The last primate stands on the shore

A steel fish net curled between his knuckles.
His toe claws the wet mush, leaving furrows

Like the rusted automated tractors churning
With the enduring determineless determination

Of the machine's complex simplicity.
They will batter the earth as long as their batteries last.

He casts his net and collects the permanent bric-a-brac.
He does so from day into Byronic darkness.

He squirms his tongue's worm into shells
And holds the spittled cockle to his ears.

There are no howling demons left to fear;
No gods to give black jackal or wicked panther godheads.

The black stripes of tigers consumed the white
And orange flame; gone as the need

For fireside, huddle, and cave.
And what lives are the oldest dead:

The plastic dinosaurs of the permanent amusement park
Further down the pier.

Beneath their outstretched moonlit sickle shapes
The only swallows are the bites of frost.

He pulls his final teeth. His bones will outlast
His hunger, and feed the invisible.

The new Adam, with nothing left to name.

THE GREY RHINO

For Christine Hill's 'Black Rhinoceros' statue, Great North Museum
As a silhouette
Writ in soot.
  — Ted Hughes, *The Black Rhino*

I put my lips to the horn on the hill.
I see the ghost through the charge's dust.

Let spit animate the trumpet
Of the stomp, the snort, the shout.

The scuttle of legs like treads bringing
The turret, the rumble, and the armour

To a war as lost as you from time and home.
An older and ruined castle tumbled here.

Eye, a tree knot to show your age,
A family tree with long roots under stumps.

Horn, a scimitar blunt to wounds,
A crescent shadow, a chunk of chitin fallen moon.

A saddle for the agile, blind to the sign and the rock,
The child feels the savannah's quick heat through the stone.

I have seen you dusted in snow;
When the last of you is silent dust

They will put you inside with the other bones,
A note pinned to your unblown horn:

Odd-toed ungulate, inanimate, a charge to see you,
A gaggle, a rush, a dip in visitors

When you cohabit with more ancient predators.

Or a dip in the pocket, a donation like an organ,
A low note to join the keratin alarum.

For your extinction
You exist

A sound
Cast in stone.

UNTITLED, THE FOURTH MONSTER[2]

I

Howay, I'll speak no new famous phrase,
Let no word of the hoard be raised above

The sunk slinkers haven, the creature's reach, the keeper's
Keep, to vile king, plunder seeker, or lippy Viking tavern.

The hag's lair is dank and thankful empty,
But for bog treasure trove and lank slithy.

Prithee, I'll tell no tales but to the tiled vault and blank
Returning smiles of skulking and insentient reptiles,
And the slick remains of my headless Yorick.

A lad, damn that I knew him
And the soft hacky look of his skullet.

My boy's muggish skull, open and taken from the gill
To the froth and gore of Hrothgar's hall and shelter,

---

2   A scrap of singed parchment containing this poem was
found at Ashburnham House following the 1731 fire that charred the
margins of the sole surviving *Beowulf* manuscript. I was allowed to view
a transcription of this text by the current holder, under promise of utmost
secrecy, however from the transcription (which I quickly memorised for
publication here) we can infer that several scribes have been at work, likely
successive archivists, due to anachronistic and stylistic quirks. Admittedly, I
left it a little late to record what I had seen, following a short nap brought
on by an excess of refreshment and poetry, however I am confident in my
abilities of recall, following former Education Secretary Michael Gove's
wildly successful 2012 educational diktat concerning poetic memorisation
and recitation, which has induced sufficient rigour to my powers of
recollection.

An old ruin, who servants call the Shieldings' helmet.

Taken! By ill met Beowulf, bearish wolfish mutt,
Shining swimming codpiece of the Geat armoury.

My poor bairn, become right hand of the king, pinned
And heltered, shouldering the barn eaves for his barney.

And now his limb hangs and high fives heroes,
And the slappers tax the longevity of taxidermy
And I count down the fallen fingers to zero.

For where nothing is, I am.

For every monster there's a critic.

II

This is my boast:

I am the enemy of fame and thane.

I am the silence Heardred dreaded more
Than the king who stole his line.

I am what Hygelac's high kinsman lacked.
The son of Ecgtheow's low unheard echo.

The fourth monster, the thirteenth man,
The third murderer, a thief, and the miscounted.

The unsexed dint of Unferth's blunt blade.
The spider in the web of your war-shirt.

My coat is patched with the plain back of tapestries.

I'll hack and molest his bones to less than dust
With impish claws, and melt away like a giant's sword.

Hunt me, Hrunt me, but you'll never find me!
Rank warrior, I am the unintelligible grunt, the unknown soldier.

The living deadbeat dad of the beaten son,
Husband to the hag, a lag, a gag, a bad lad,
Tagged and permanently It.

The demon dementia, the ruler in absentia.
I think and am not.

Anon, a nothing, a no one, the cane to spit
The eye from your head, and roll the boulder
To shush the cave's mouth.

Nameless, I took my wife's name when I married her,
She'll turn on the spindle, roast in gamy hell for this betrayal:
A mother's love, the naming of lame and unlamented Grendel.

III

So, the geet big git got his title.

Word has reached me, and my smudge named boat

Has met the breakers and been burnt for smoke and firewood.

The years have been kind to you, and you a king to them.
You tell tall stories, and your back bends.

What that old man would give to grapple
With Grendel's mother's cousin's son,

Whoever he can get his honeyed paws on,
And twice remove an arm, a leg, a head.

He plunders his own life, like a confessional poet, desperate
Of sins and stories, he'll leave himself with nothing, separate

The legend from the man and I'll feast
On the mess and clart of his cleft nothingness.

IV

At night, I lie on his barrow, a fortress
Festooned in forget me nots, and vow

To be your last bedfellow; Wiglaf has wilted,
His skull shows his mirth, and I wear the grass to baldest earth,
Staring out over the coast, locking my teeth,

To the rising glasses of imagined toasts,
And the falling voices of recited boasts.

So, king, your bones are smoke,
But, I will not wait for the rot of parchment:

I will unman the manuscript

And leave your tombed treasure cross with my X.

ENGLISH SOCIOPATH, OR, THE INSIDES OF A CUFFLINK BOX, AND OTHER CONTENTMENTS

He sewed it on so neatly,
the seam was never seen.
  — *Sing a Song of Sixpence*

Within two steps of his bed, a brown leather Dulwich cufflink box with deliberate pale stitches shares a shelf, sandwiched between stacks of books and identical aftershave bottles. Inside, cufflinks neatly paired or doubled up sets in sections. Contents. One is of a Van Gogh painting. Another Turner. *The Fighting Temeraire* sinks next to swirling stars and bending night. He mixes and matches his Napoleon and Wellington portrait sets, so an observant onlooker, skilled at the interpretation of signs, birds in the air, blood of beasts on the ground, and the ilk, would know: the blood of his wrists are at war with each other. Of topical use also whenever his country spats with France. Further contents: a novelty pair his Dad bought him as half a joke for the London twenty twelve mayoral campaign (at eighteen or nineteen, not so many years after his first deliberate shirt). He has never lived in London. In the succeeding years his father has grown to hate Johnson. The Boris cufflinks are shelved, in extreme likelihood indefinitely. Further contents. Two silver stags, another present from the same man, this one requested and without humour. On his wrists they scrape like chariot wheels. Their antlers are all twisted with his name. They are the most expensive in his collection. They also take up the most room. They live in brown pens besides the wisdom of owls, the folly of kings, a fixed compass point, and, uncirculated, a set of sixpences. They live in brown pens besides the eternity of waters, the scarcity of pearls, and the never of dragons. He does not know what he will do when the last slot is full and he has no room for others. He supposes he will stop. He will not buy another container. Most of the shirts he owns now are sadly button cuff. His favourite brands keep going out of business.

Behind the box a dark skinned desk tidy (John Lewis) full of theatre tickets.

Nightstand. In matching leather a valet tray – same deliberate Dulwich pale stitches – his watch goes in and out of. His watch: white face, gold bezel, brown leather strap, gold accoutrements. Powered by the movements of his body. He thinks this is a better measure of time than the arbitrary cycles of moon, and earth, and work, and women and sun. It runs out a lot. He sleeps long hours, is rarely interested in morning. Further contents: gold signet ring he will one day inscribe with a wife's name. Oval face, half slash indeterminate pattern. Vaguely florid imitation aristocratic. An untidy stack of shirt collar stiffeners like a jumble of bad directions. Note: should replace with single set. Silver slash gold.

Within 16 inches of the tray three cheap alarm clocks. He is slumberous, generally in morning incapacitate. He has two other notable timepieces. One, a large front hanging like a dark pure lake, silver shored, stopped deliberate at permanent twelve. Another, smaller, with a chain and a box, also two handed against the hour. The latter is the oldest of his accomplishments. The least looked at. He feels like his hands have only been conscious from the moment they twisted and fixed the crown to their liking.

On the same shelf as the cufflinks, boxed: a silver tie clip and polishing cloth. There are several symbols on it. He cannot recall what the man in the shop told him they meant – something about the derivation and purity of the metal. For once this increases his enjoyment. If asked, he will improvise.

He owns a great many ties, of many pleasing patterns, plainnesses, and insignias. However, his wardrobe door is mostly closed, and he cannot see into it from the cushion of his bed or the concentration of his desk – so he cannot name them. He does remember that some patterns predate their meanings. Example: lions he liked before he attended his local university and met the spread claws, flung mane, and stuck out tongue of the campus mascot.

He has two, maybe three, lapel pins, somewhere out of sight. Yes, three, an Olympian array: gold, and other metals. He would like more. He has yet to find an occasion to wear one. He envies politicians and their easy choices. Their assigned flags and NHS badges. The Americans have it even better, the intricate psychopathic pins of congress and senate.

He still carries the ten year old wallet despite multiple subsequent birthdays and Christmas presents from parents, grandma, and more distant relations. He keeps them in a drawer, unused. After a suitable time has passed, discards. The wallet he pockets is black on the outside, brilliant red on the inside. Still looks expensive. A Fortnum & Mason present from his mother. Tattered in places. Launer. By royal appointment, though this contradicts his most dearly held political principle. Inside there is his twelve years out of date under sixteen bus pass. On the picture he is even younger, his face purpled by poor optical technology. He wonders what would happen if he tried to use it.

He has gone through several iterations of brown leather belts with chunky square silver buckles. They wear out too quickly. Current model: Hugo Boss, soon in need of replacement. He enjoys the deliberate concrete border between his tucked in shirt and the black groin and twin lines of his jeans. To this ensemble, no variations. Jacket: weather dependant. Suit or smart long. Low weight blazer for when there is a suffusion of excess light. His body temperature is high, so he needs no surfeit of additional layers and despises those who do – and worse over accessorise.

Shoes wear out too quickly. Worse than belts. He still remembers the time the man in the shop tutted at the state of his. Corbyn made news for the same reason, their disrepair. He (the owner of the worn shoes) is heavy on his feet. He should have bought enough pairs that one time previous, so he never had to iterate again. He dislikes slippers and wellington boots. They make him fall over. And his slow deliberate movements cannot help.

He has several dreams, this is part way towards one of them. One eye half open the dragon sleeps empty-bellied amidst his treasure hoard.

An armour of scale and coins.

He has black feathers, a dark beak, a streak of turquoise that allies him with the water, eyes like pools for silver swords to live inside.

Everything else he owns is just the usual thicket of branches and bramble and junk that make a nest. He has named all of his treasures, like Adam standing in the long grass, waiting for the serpent to talk.

ACEDIA

I

Though the journey is short
It is still a squeezing of wheels and metal and onrushing air,

Of paper printed and deformed under the thunk
Of punched holes and scrutinized under lasers.

But after the revolution and small tumult of ringed keys,
And the peeling and resealing of a door from its frame

There is a place where the air is still.
Where the turning of the chains and metal snag

Make the mechanic grip relent,
Chew and snap a virtue out of vice,

Like the torn hairs shed daily
With my wrist device and manacle.

And without time's revolutions I am free to unevolve
Into my former species:

To transform the blue lizard scale of a week's work
To the verdant fur that stretches brown and slowly out

Beneath now bulbous eyes blind to daylight
Above a dark mouth widening into smacking lips.

Fingernails worn down to nubs by fast clacking
Yawn into long claws that curl and balance

A whole body's shaggy weight in easeful tension.

II
Weightless and sinless without the care of body

The human ghost settles into a place of dust
Like a cadaver in his bunk.

The new life will rise with the season for cleaning.
But for now spring is far away, and dreams are close.

Two times out of seven, the sum of sun becomes
All day afternoons and the absence of mornings.

III
The sleeper leaves hair uncombed and fit for magpies
To nest and pick silver threads for slow weaving

Into the whorl of small houses
To baby perfect thoughts.

And when the doorway is unsealed like an airlock,
Or the wax that keeps a letter, remember

There is a place where the air is still enough
To be maneuvered by the softness of my breathing.

THE YOUNG MARINER

Had I from old and young
— Samuel Taylor Coleridge, *The Rime of the Ancient Mariner*

The world is just an albatross
With a human round its neck.

At the funeral, she speaks with gritted teeth.

We wore away the soft ruff and hard rachis,
Our arms stretched wide, our legs straight, like a dangling crucifix

On a plastic string that neither of us could snap
By tooth or beak.

We broke the horrid silence of the sea.
We ran aground and splashed black paint beneath blue braes.

We broke and kept on breaking
Until Inanimate-lived-in-Animate.

The parched Polar Spirit wisps away.
He licks his lips to speak; he thought the polar opposite.

The casket closes.
She loses his attention.

"I'm the damned pallbearer."
He rubs a cracked nail over an aching shoulder.

He rests the wooden chute on his slick black suit.
Through the crematorium grate waits a nation of ash and smoke.

They lumber on
Like dead men tugging at the rigging.

With a tired step
He sets the sun close over tomorrow's morning.

THE DREAM OF METHUSELAH
The vapours weep their burthen to the ground
— Alfred, Lord Tennyson, *Tithonus*

He never really died. So old they mistook him for dead.
His coffin will rot before he does. Floated out across infinite waters.

The damp wood, all that they could spare
From their awed Ark building.

So old his sagging skin and toothless mouth
Have come back into fashion.

Fashioned from a more durable clay
Than the rest of us.

When his body is just cells he will still live,
Only in a smaller prison.

And stuck beneath the soil when the waves
And wails his father prophesied have receded

He dreams. And this was his dream:

The human ghost ascended to a silver shadowed shape,
Wet flesh shed and exchanged for the cranial juices
That live effeminate among the clouds;
Black cattle and white lambs boiled down
To finish a flood's work, and scald the feet of giants:
The gods recalled themselves to the shadow worlds of death.
Bones grown on a mutant crop, sucked dry
And discarded like comrades in a Cyclops's cave.

Pestilence unhorsed by a syringe's javelin jab,
Famine starved to death by the absence of stomachs,
And himself, long lived enough to witness: the death of the sword.

The beard of a god and oceans have wisped away,
And all that lives in the dry heat that remains
Is a brain so slick memories glide right off.
And everything is met with no knowledge, but pretended familiarity.
And the only tastes are the tastes of earliest youth:
Snatches of songs long marinated on the tongue, and the sting of apple.
Powerless now even to remember the body's first quick defeat.
And his own coffin skin in bloom, long nurtured by a nameless earth,
Stretching a tower towards the sky.

And the reader will flick back to the first pages
And the black book's long genealogies,
And leave her bookmark there.

And one day the airy beings will stoop down,
And scoop him from the silt, their first forebearer.

To see the toothless, mouthless, memory devoid grin
Gaping uglier than hell. Methuselah, he will outlive them all.

SCRAPS TO DAUB A SIREN'S LIPS

Siren, your lips are living laurels;
From them I was born.

Put these dead leaves to the hectic red
And leave me the cartography of the lines
Of beauty that live on your ancient lips.

The swollen kingdom of the vermillion border.

The divine counterpart to the human
Palm line from which we divine and sign

Our futures.

They move like under ocean currents
Hard to trace with eye or hand.

I still hold your fallen feather in mine,
Balanced between thumb and forefinger.

Tickled by the soft stroke
Of sea slick plumology.

I swim in salt waters.
I must learn to drink from them again.

Mine is the way of the fish,
Battered and wrapped in paper printed

With all my poetry.

My only thought
The isle, the isle, the isle.

The land that lives within your garland.

To-morrow, I will tell you how I will get there.

ACKNOWLEDGEMENTS

With thanks to the editors of the following magazines, newspapers, and anthologies, for the first publication of some of the poems found in this collection: *Abridged*, Acid Bath Publishing's *Travels & Tribulations* anthology, *Amethyst Review*, Black Bough Poetry's *Freedom Rapture* anthology, *Blackbox Manifold*, *Crannóg*, *Finished Creatures*, *Fly on the Wall Press Magazine*, *The Honest Ulsterman*, *Chasing Shadows*, *The London Magazine*, *The Mechanics' Institute Review*, Newcastle University's *One Planet Anthology* (published as part of the university's Alumni Day of Action), *New Contrast*, *The New European*, *Perverse*, *Poetry Birmingham Literary Journal*, *Poetry Bus*, *Poetry Salzburg Review*, *Poetry Scotland*, *Prairie Fire*, *Rewilding: An Ecopoetic Anthology*, *ROPES Literary Journal*, *The Seventh Quarry*, *Shearsman*, *Southword*, *Streetcake Magazine*, *The Storms*, the University of Oxford's *A Tapestry of Homes: An Anthology* (published as part of the A Personal History of Home project by The Oxford Research Centre in the Humanities), *Visual Verse*, *Wild Court*, and *York Literary Review*. Particular thanks to Suna Afshan for her editing of 'Nine Spilt Yolks' for *Poetry Birmingham Literary Journal*.

The prose poem reviews included in the collection were commended in the National Centre for Writing's UEA New Forms Award 2021. Earlier versions of the collection were shortlisted for the Cinnamon Press Poetry Pamphlet Award 2022, and longlisted for the Cinnamon Press Poetry Pamphlet Prize 2021.

I was commissioned to write 'The Last Animal' for the Ilkley Literature Festival 2022 for National Poetry Day, as one of the festival's New Northern Poets. The poem was part of the festival strand 'The Things We Leave Behind'. 'Prose / Poem' was shortlisted for the Streetcake Experimental Writing Prize 2019, poetry category. 'I Haunt You Back (A Prose Poem Book Review of *Surge* by Jay Bernard)', was one of the winners of the Shortlist Book Review Competition 2020, held in celebration of the Dylan Thomas Prize by Swansea University, and was first published on the Swansea University website.

I am also grateful to the Ilkley Literature Festival New Northern Poets, BBC New Creatives, and New Writing North North East Poets schemes for supporting my development as a poet, and to the below poets and publishers for granting permission to include the quotations within the collection.

I am immensely grateful to Broken Sleep Books for publishing *New Famous Phrases*, and to Aaron Kent for editing the collection. And finally, special thanks to my twin brother, Craig, for being the first reader of all of the poems in this book.

LAY OUT YOUR UNREST

www.ingramcontent.com/pod-product-compliance
Ingram Content Group UK Ltd.
Pitfield, Milton Keynes, MK11 3LW, UK
UKHW041452090525
458351UK00018B/98